THE FILM SCORE COLLECTION

CONTENTS

— PIANO LEVEL —
LATE INTERMEDIATE/EARLY ADVANCED

ISBN 978-1-4234-6221-7

HAL•LEONARD®
CORPORATION
7777 W. BLUEMOUND RD. P.O. BOX 13819 MILWAUKEE, WI 53213

Visit Hal Leonard Online at
www.halleonard.com

Visit Phillip at
www.phillipkeveren.com

THEME FROM E.T.
(THE EXTRA-TERRESTRIAL)

from the Universal Picture E.T. (THE EXTRA-TERRESTRIAL)

Music by JOHN WILLIAMS
Arranged by Phillip Keveren

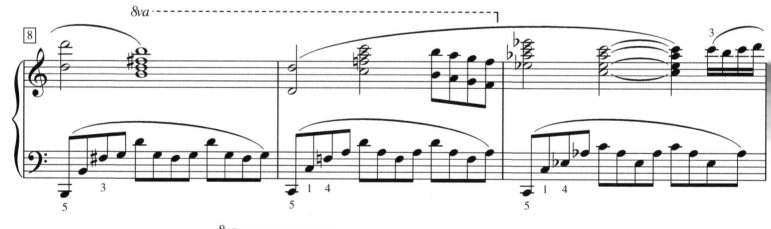

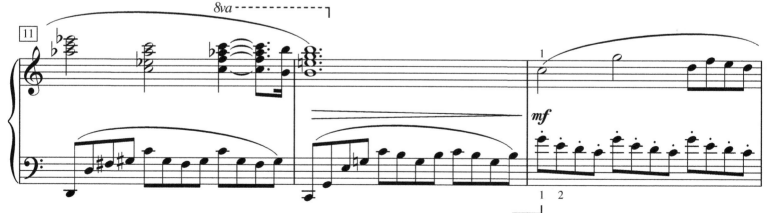

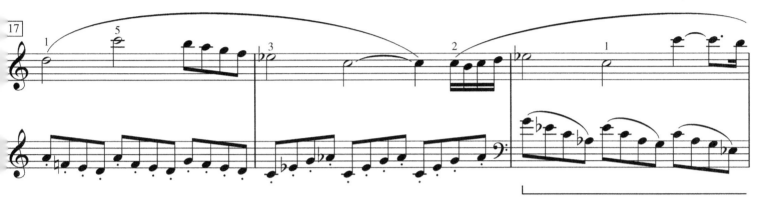

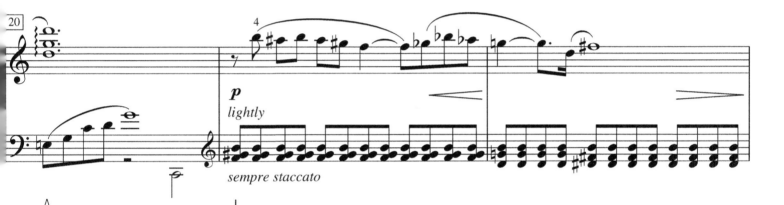

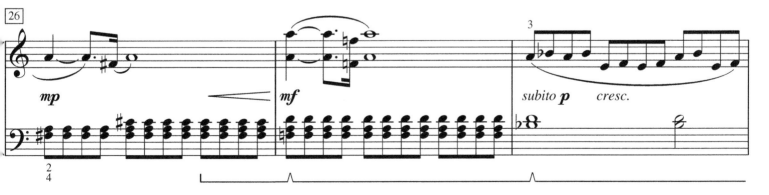

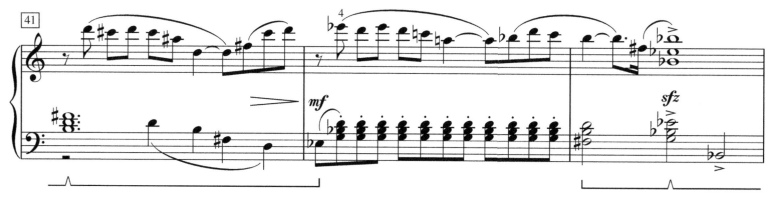

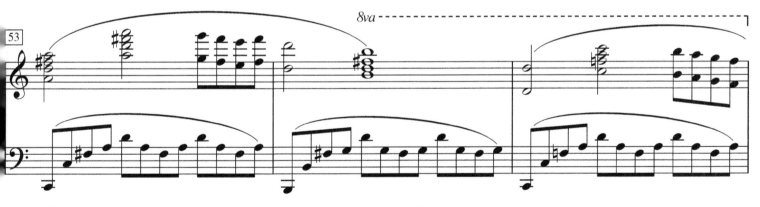

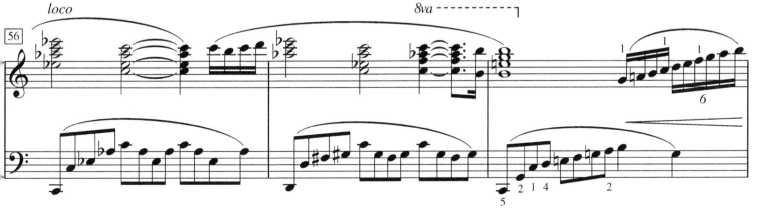

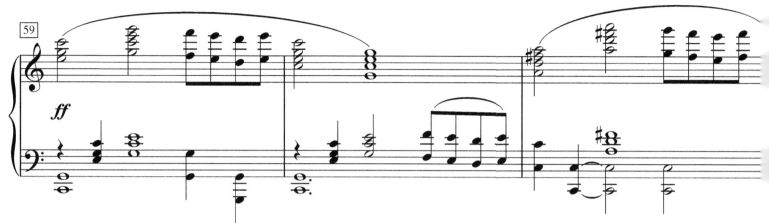

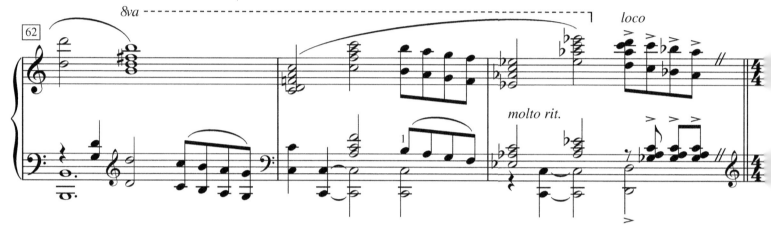

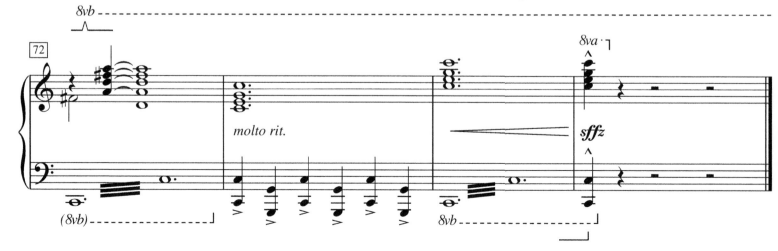

FORREST GUMP – MAIN TITLE
(Feather Theme)
from the Paramount Motion Picture FORREST GUMP

Music by ALAN SILVESTRI
Arranged by Phillip Keveren

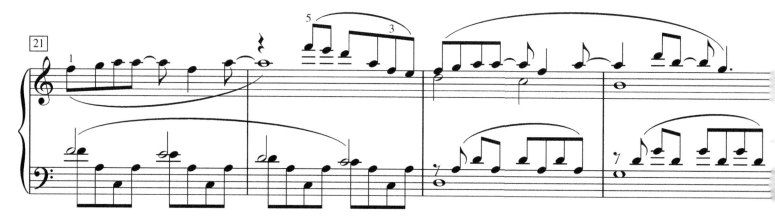

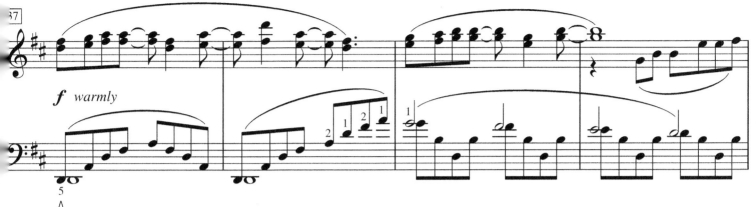

f warmly

mf

p

dim. e rit.

pp

GABRIEL'S OBOE
from the Motion Picture THE MISSION

Words and Music by
ENNIO MORRICONE
Arranged by Phillip Keveren

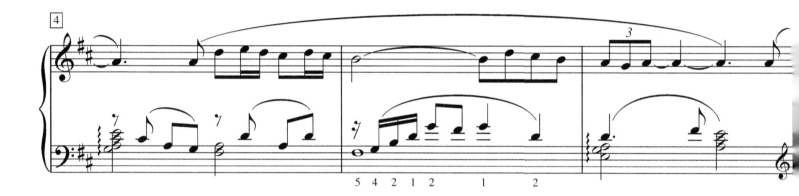

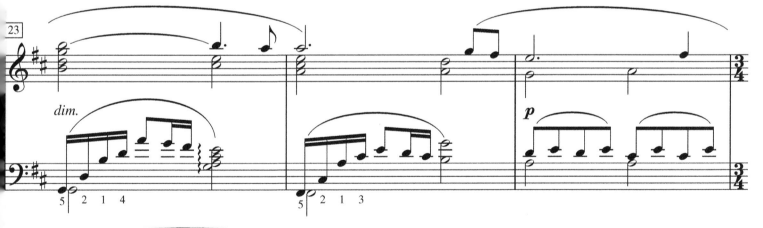

GHOST
Theme from the Paramount Motion Picture GHOST

By MAURICE JARRE
Arranged by Phillip Keveren

Flowing, expressively (♩ = 84)

With pedal

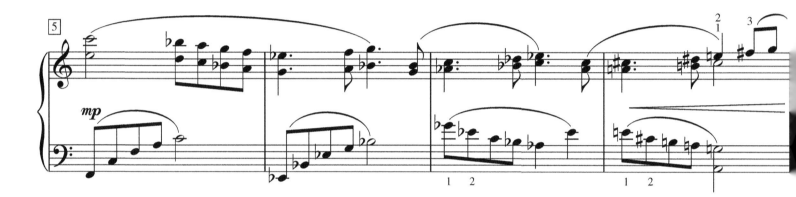

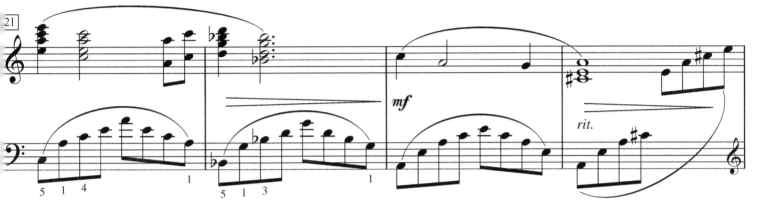

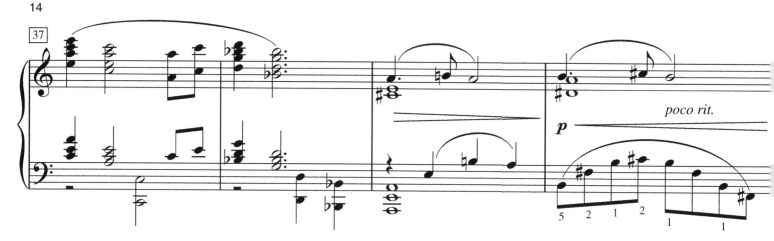

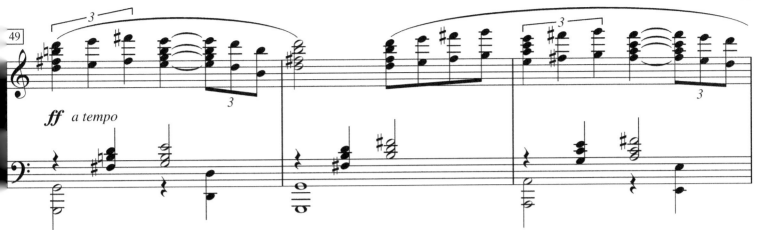

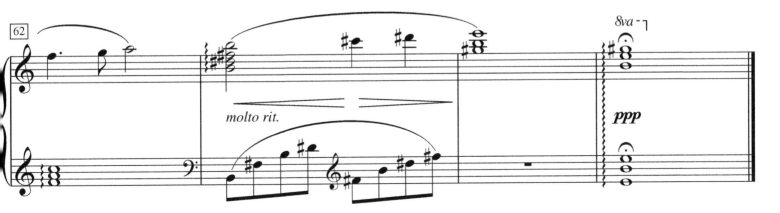

GODFATHER II
Theme from the Paramount Picture GODFATHER II

By NINO ROTA
Arranged by Phillip Keveren

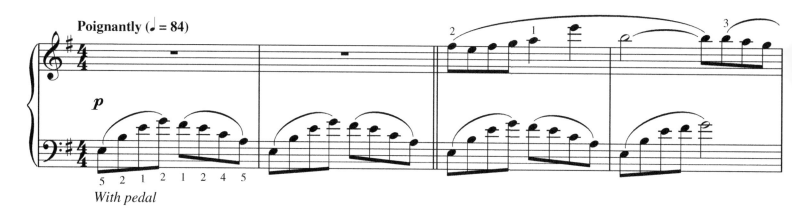

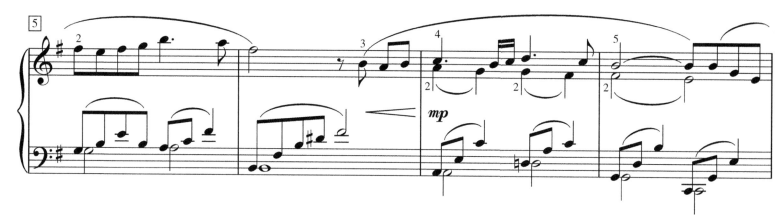

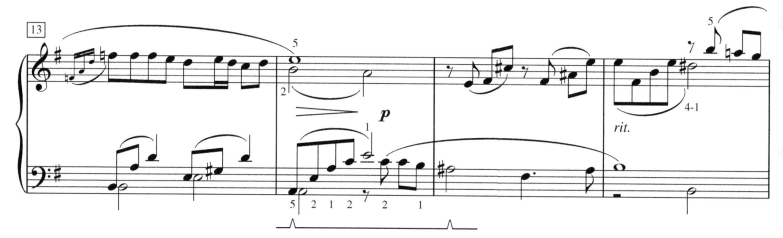

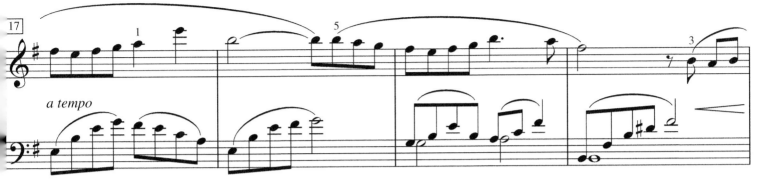

a tempo

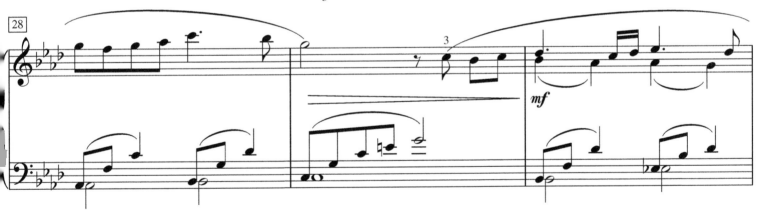

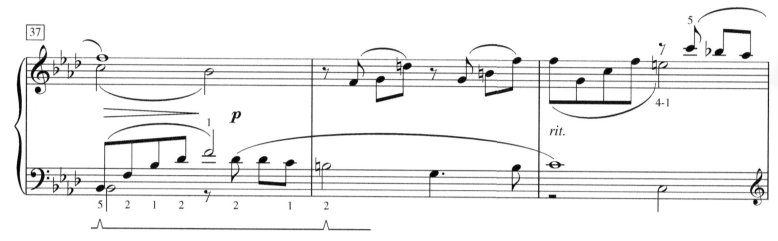

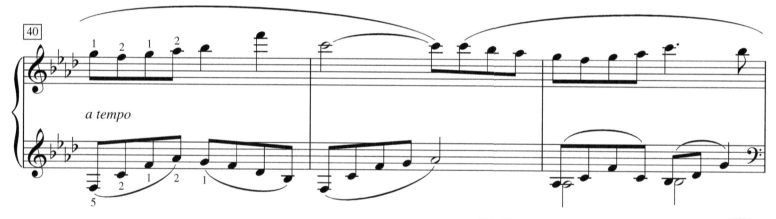

HEAVEN CAN WAIT
(Love Theme)
from the Paramount Motion Picture HEAVEN CAN WAIT

Music by DAVE GRUSIN
Arranged by Phillip Keveren

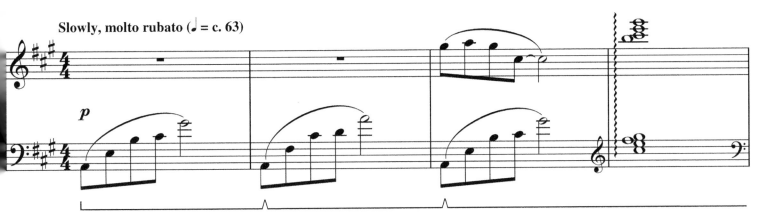

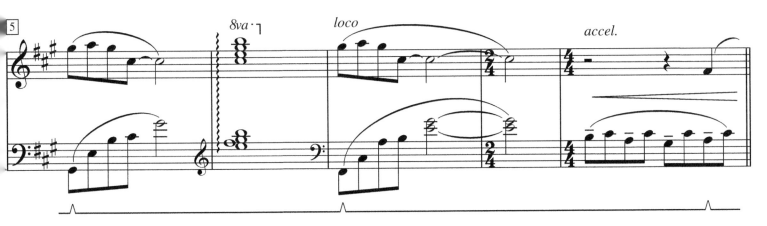

Slowly, molto rubato

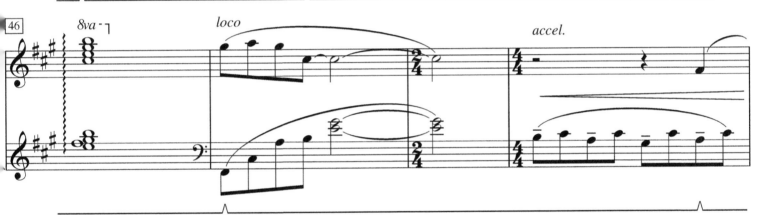

Flowing (♩ = 80)

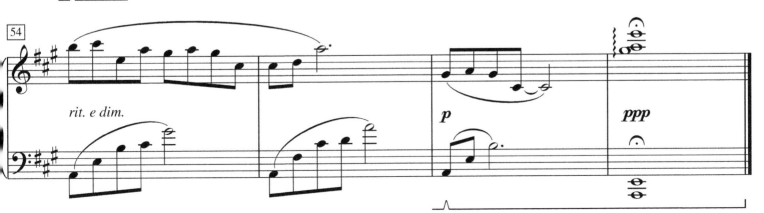

IL POSTINO
(The Postman)
from IL POSTINO

Music by LUIS BACALOV
Arranged by Phillip Keveren

Passionately, with rubato ($\quad$ = c. 72)

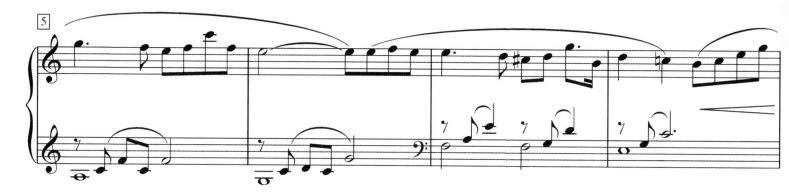

With pedal

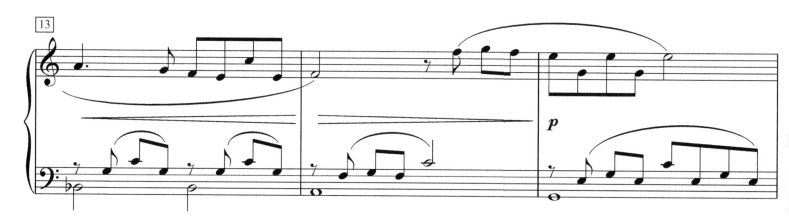

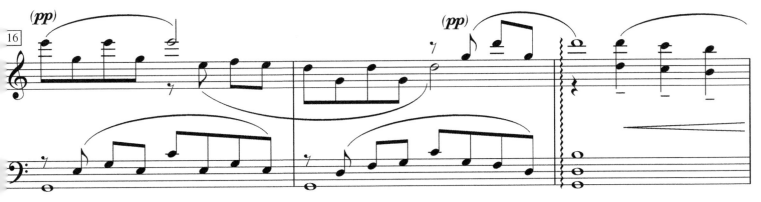

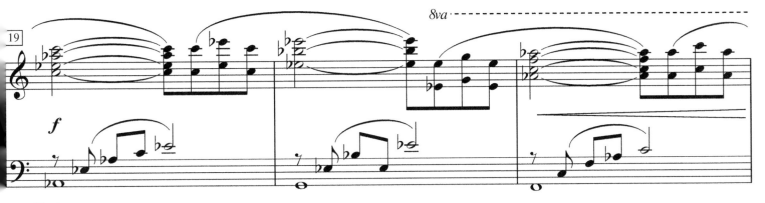

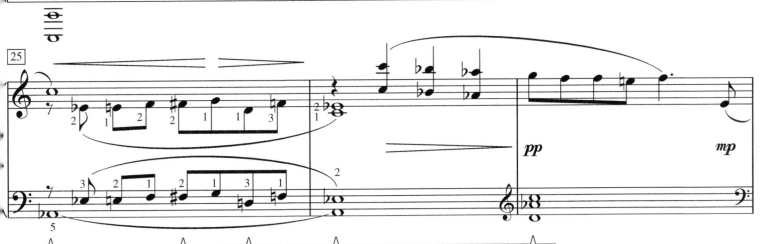

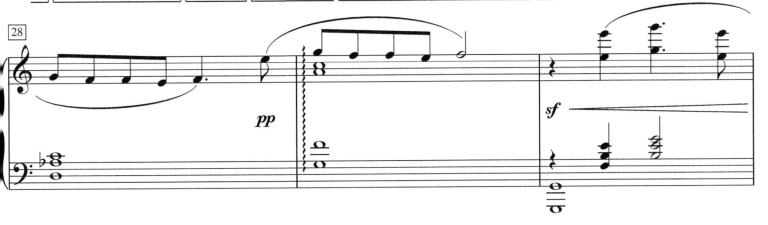

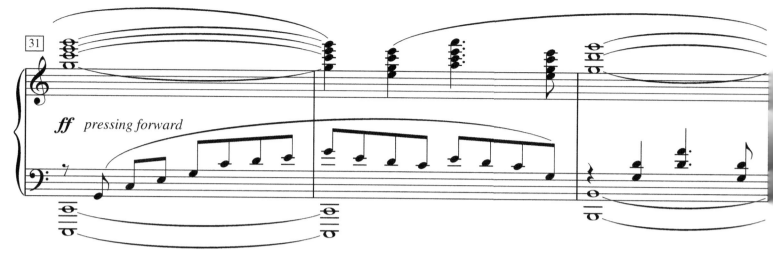

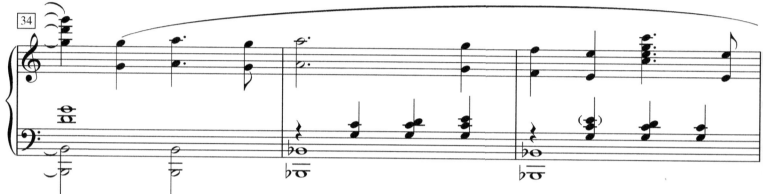

LEGENDS OF THE FALL

from TriStar Pictures' LEGENDS OF THE FALL

Composed by JAMES HORNER
Arranged by Phillip Keveren

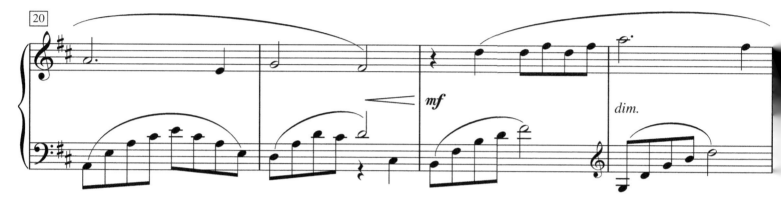

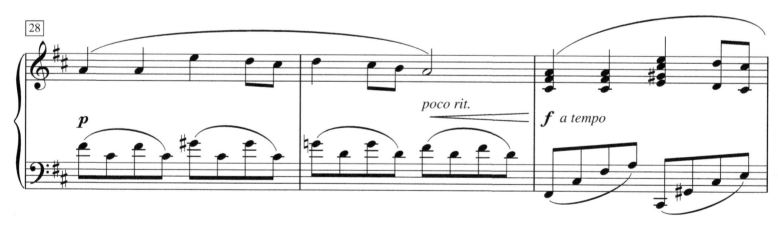

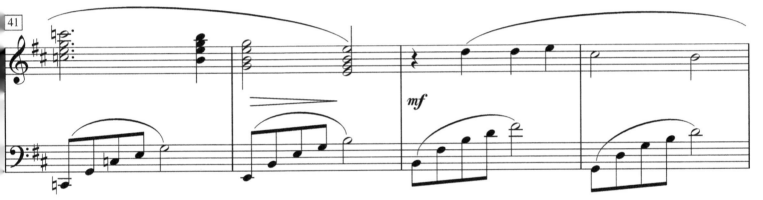

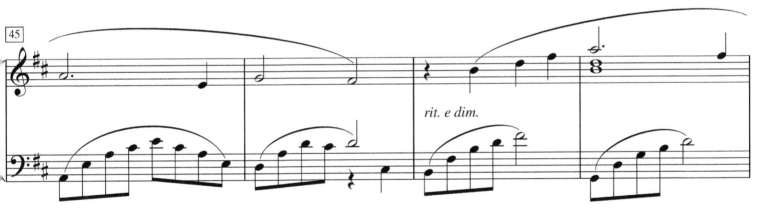

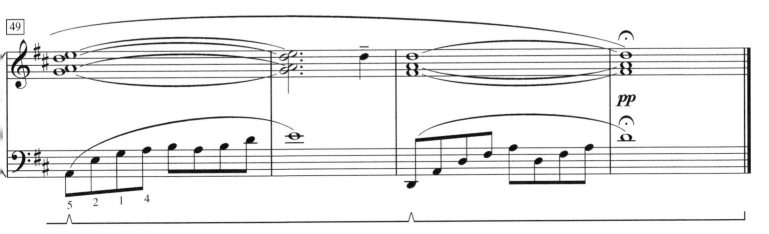

ON GOLDEN POND
Main Theme from ON GOLDEN POND

Music by DAVE GRUSIN
Arranged by Phillip Keveren

Tranquilly, molto rubato (♩ = c. 60)

With pedal

Andante rubato (♩ = c. 88)

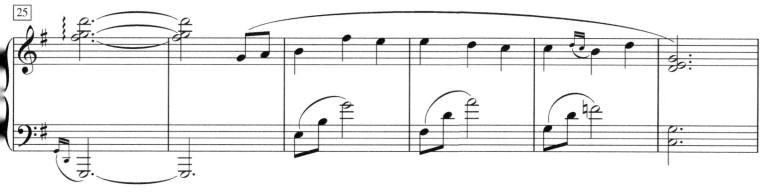

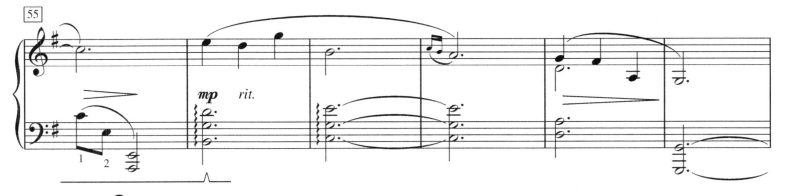

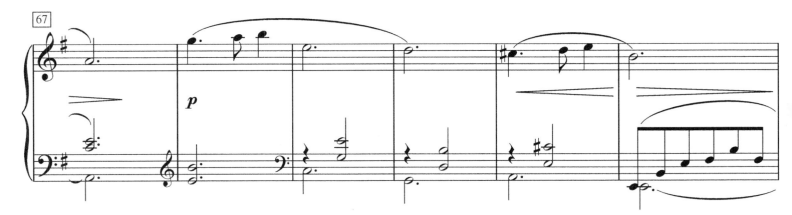

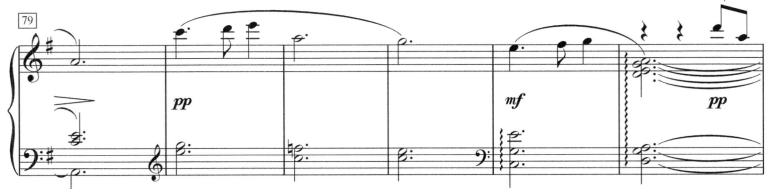

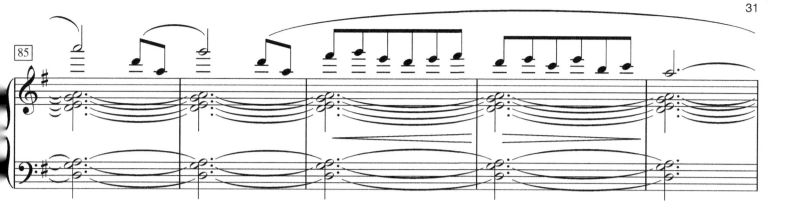

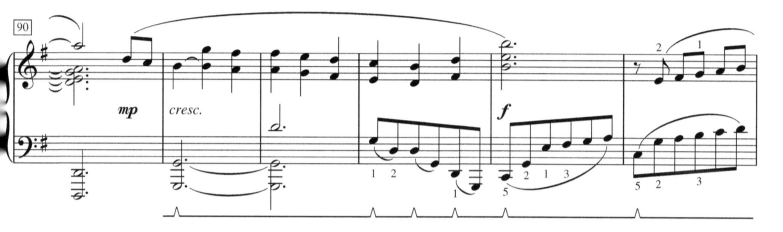

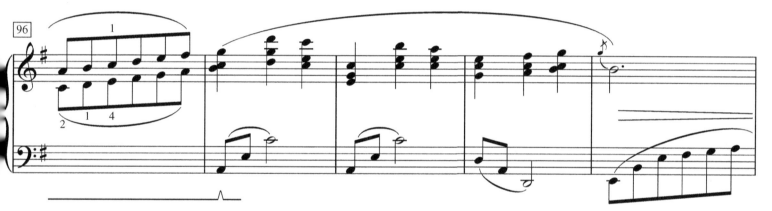

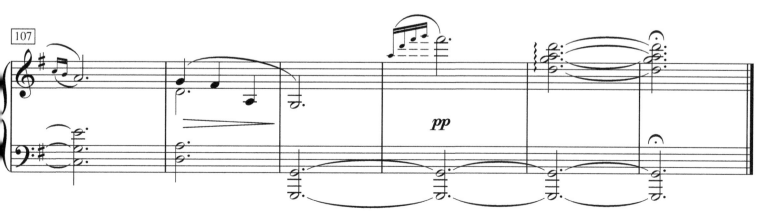

RUDY – MAIN TITLE
Theme from RUDY

Composed by JERRY GOLDSMITH
Arranged by Phillip Keveren

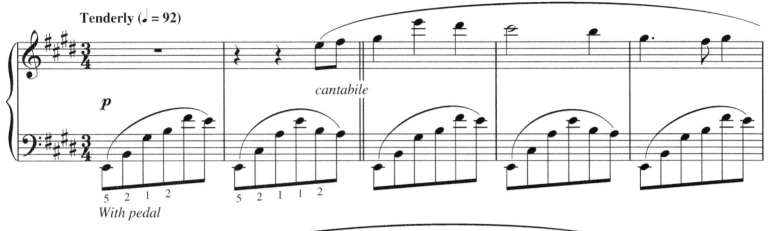

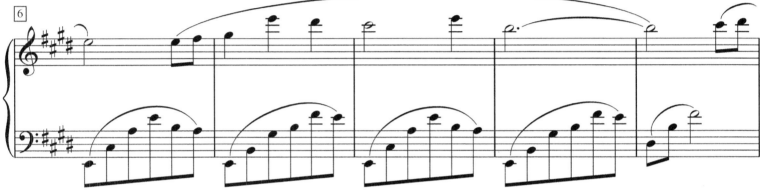

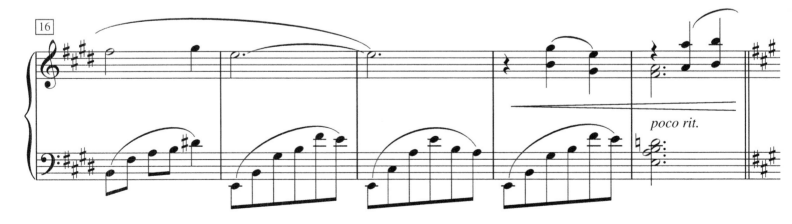

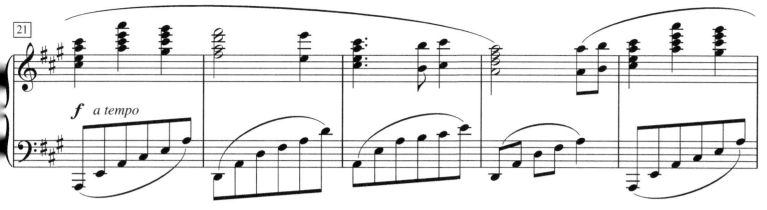

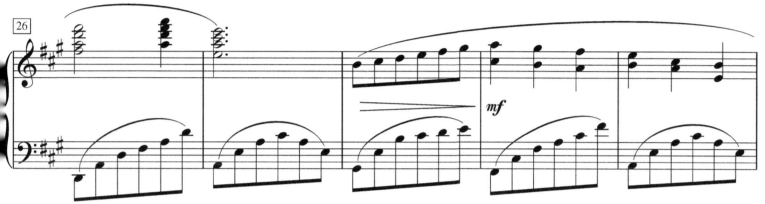

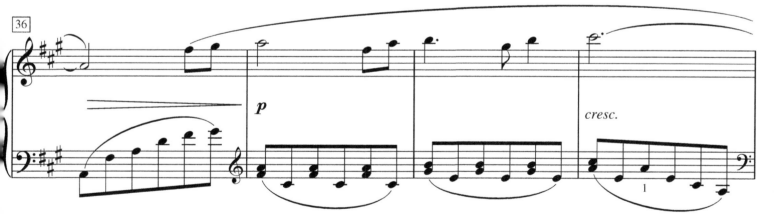

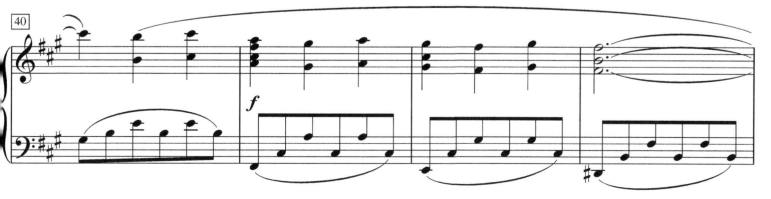

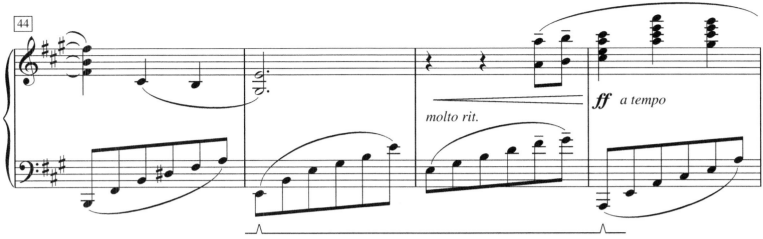

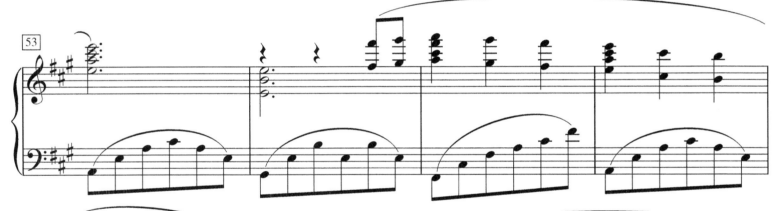

THEME FROM "SCHINDLER'S LIST"

from the Universal Motion Picture SCHINDLER'S LIST

Music by JOHN WILLIAMS
Arranged by Phillip Keveren

Slowly, deeply expressive (♩ = 56)

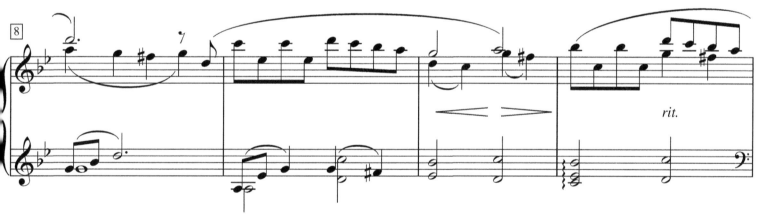

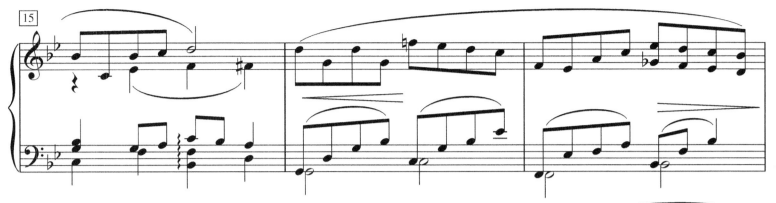

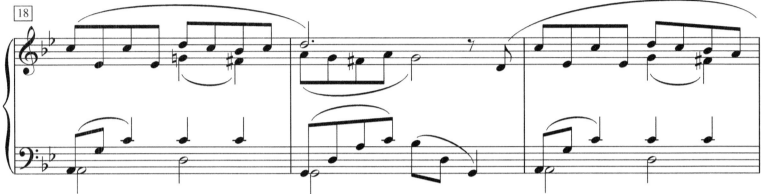

Più mosso (♩ = 63)

Tempo I

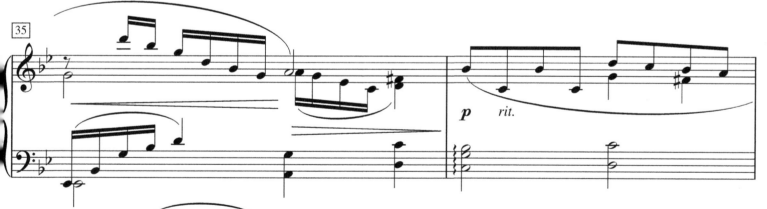

SOMEWHERE IN TIME

from SOMEWHERE IN TIME

By JOHN BARRY
Arranged by Phillip Keveren

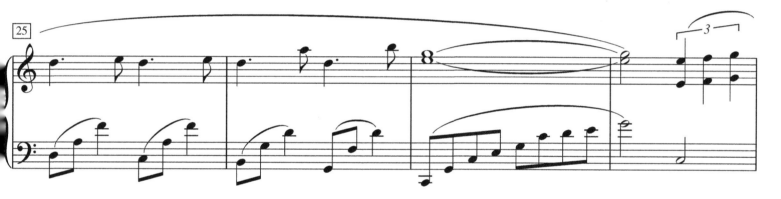

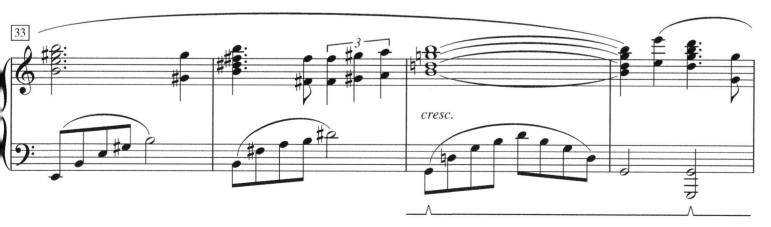

39

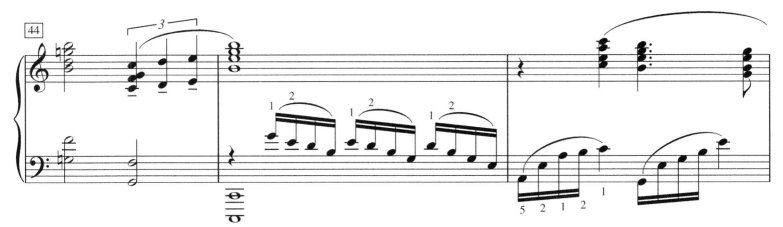

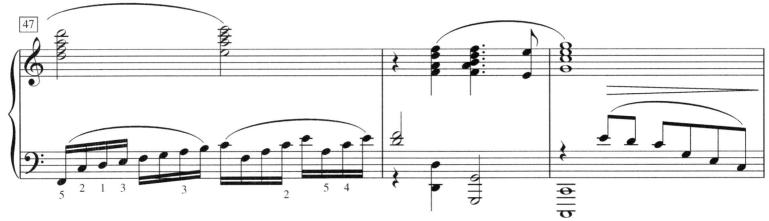

SOUTHAMPTON

from the Paramount and Twentieth Century Fox Motion Picture TITANIC

By JAMES HORNER
Arranged by Phillip Keveren

Brightly (♩ = 144)

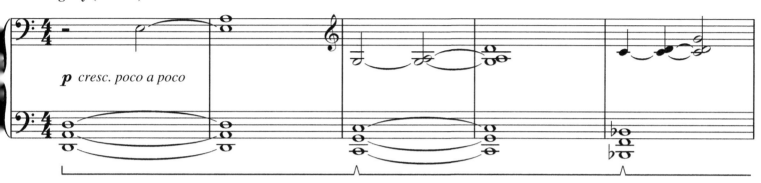

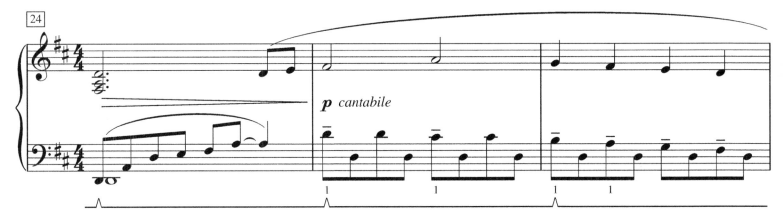

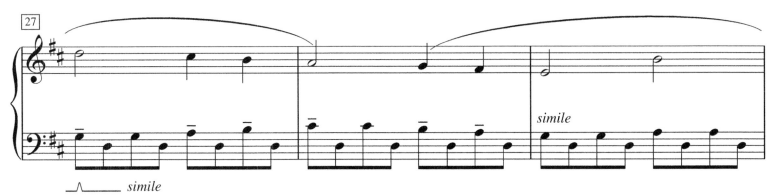

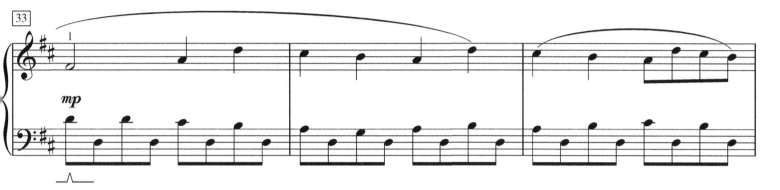

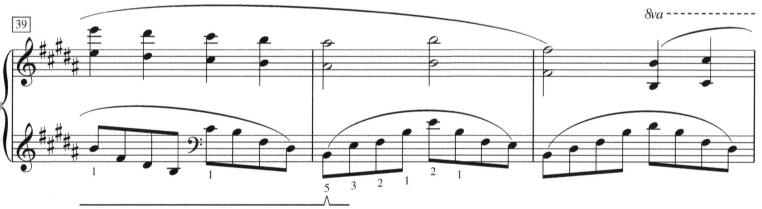

44

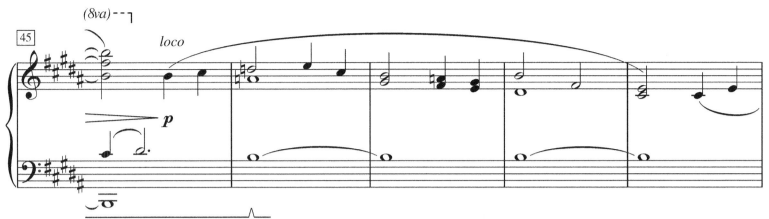

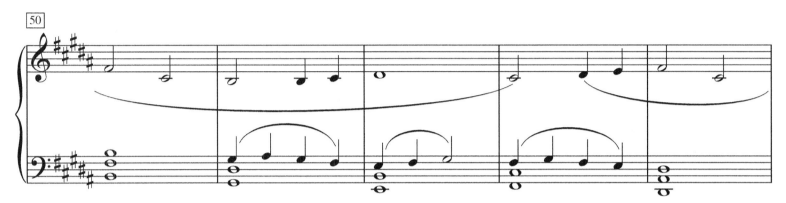

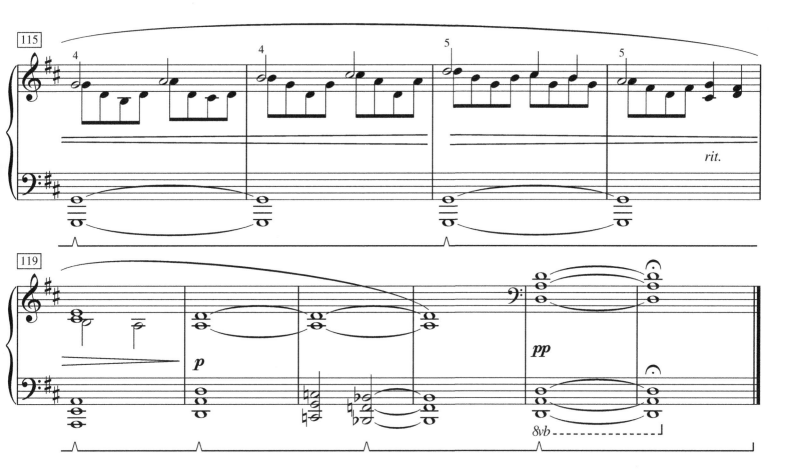

LOVE THEME FROM "ST. ELMO'S FIRE"

from the Motion Picture ST. ELMO'S FIRE

Words and Music by
DAVID FOSTER
Arranged by Phillip Keveren

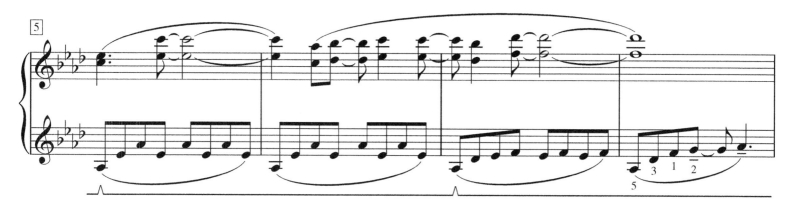

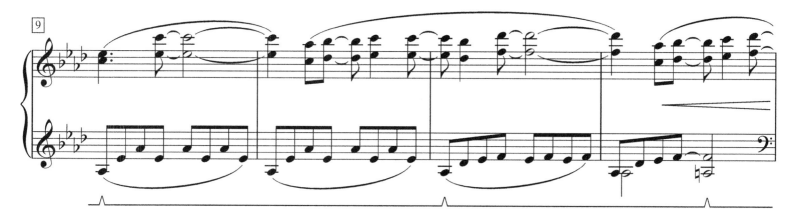

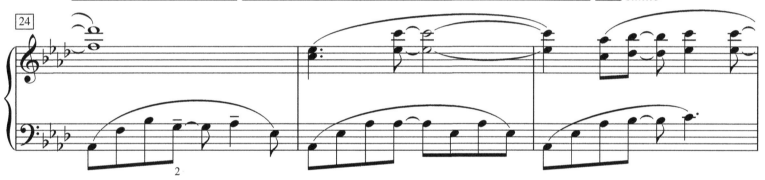

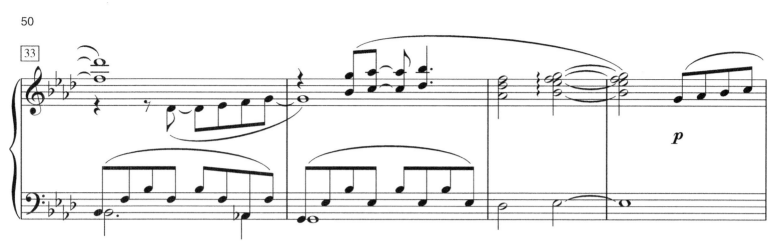

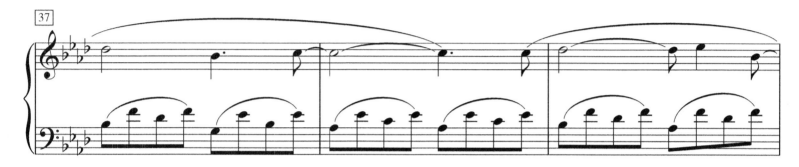

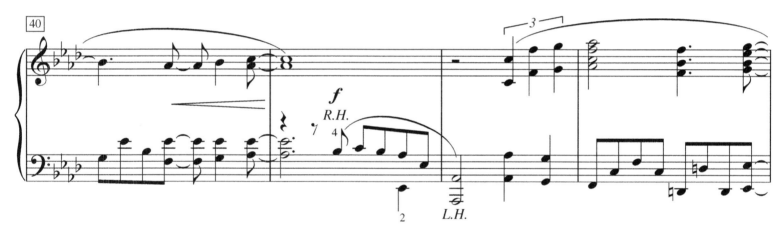

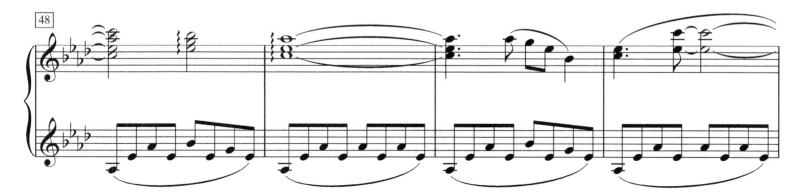

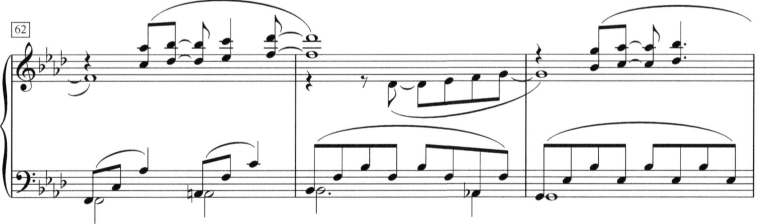

TENNESSEE

from Touchstone Pictures'/Jerry Bruckheimer Films' PEARL HARBOR

Music by HANS ZIMMER
Arranged by Phillip Keveren

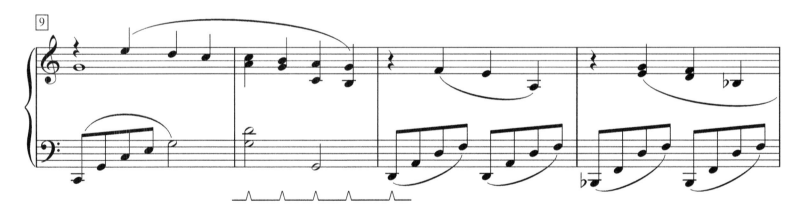

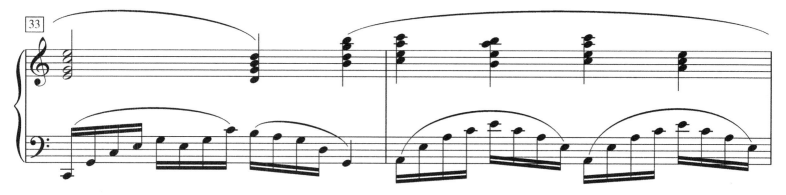

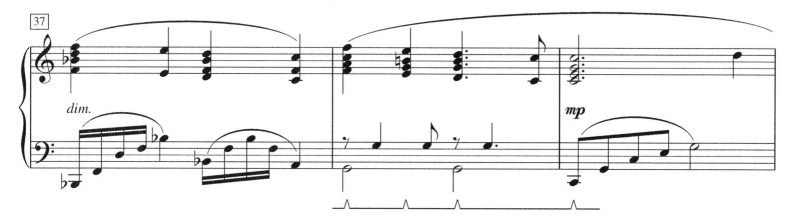

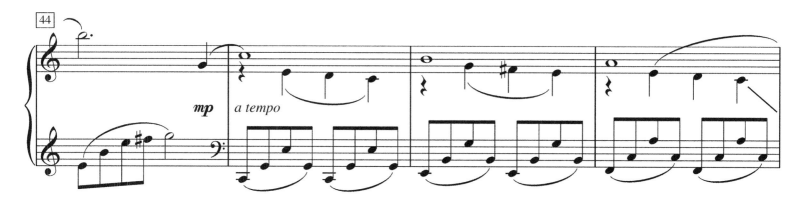

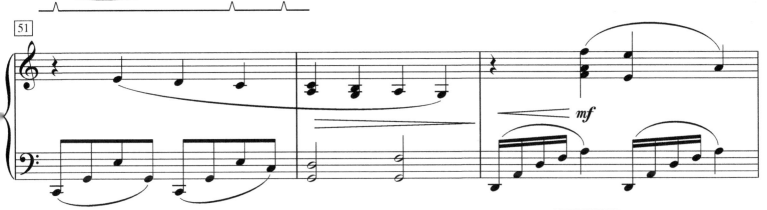

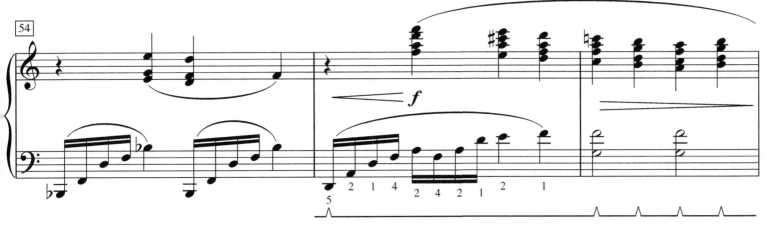

THE PHILLIP KEVEREN SERIES

HAL•LEONARD®

Search songlists, more
products and place your
order from your favorite
music retailer at
halleonard.com

Disney characters and artwork
TM & © 2021 Disney LLC

*Prices, contents, and availability
subject to change without notice.*

0422